Bright
≡Summaries.com

AF131388

The Bald Soprano

BY EUGÈNE IONESCO

BOOK ANALYSIS

Written by Delphine Leloup and Johanna Biehler

Translated by Ciaran Traynor

The Bald Soprano
by Eugène Ionesco

EUGÈNE IONESCO

FRENCH DRAMATIST

- **Born in Slatina (Romania) in 1909.**
- **Died in Paris in 1994.**
- **Notable works:**
  - *The Lesson* (1951), play
  - *Rhinoceros* (1959), play
  - *Exit the King* (1962), play

Born to a Romanian father and a French mother, Eugène Ionesco arrived in France when he was only a few years old and was made a French citizen in 1951. Although he was born in 1909, he always claimed he was born in 1912, to make himself out to be younger. His theatrical works (such as *The Bald Soprano*; *The Lesson*; *The Chairs*, 1952) left their mark on literature: today, he is one of the most performed French dramatists in the world. He wanted to make sure his works were understood, so he wrote many commentaries on them (such as *Notes and Counter Notes*, 1962; *Fragments of a Journal*, 1967). He was elected to the Académie française in 1970.

Ionesco was the leading figure of the Theatre of The Absurd, a new theatrical genre which rewrote the rules of classical theatre in the aftermath of the Second World War (1939-1945).

THE BALD SOPRANO

A DISCONCERTING WORK FROM THE THEATRE OF THE ABSURD

- **Genre**: play
- **Reference edition**: Ionesco, E. (1982) *The Bald Soprano & Other Plays*. Trans. Allen, D. New York: Grove Press.
- **1st edition**: 1950
- **Themes**: bourgeoisie, absurd, language

The short play *The Bald Soprano*, which came out in 1950, is centred around two middle-class English couples, the Martins and Smiths, whose chauvinism, way of life and social condition are all criticised by the author.

The work was branded an "anti-play" by Ionesco himself. Indeed, unlike in a traditional play, it is impossible to analyse the psychology of the characters of *The Bald Soprano* and they are interchangeable (the Martins replace the Smiths at the end of the play). Moreover, the incoherent dialogue prevents the action from progressing. The play mixes tragedy (notably with the death of Bobby Watson) with farcical situations (the Martins do not realise that they are married).

SUMMARY

An English couple, Mr. and Mrs. Smith, are sitting in an English living room. Mr. Smith is smoking an English pipe and reading an English newspaper, while Mrs. Smith is trying to make conversation.

However, what is supposed to be dialogue is actually nothing more than a monologue, since the husband is absorbed by his newspaper and does not speak, but merely clicks his tongue. Mary, the servant, then appears on stage, and she tells her employers about her recent day out. The two are more than happy to learn that she went to the cinema with a man to watch a film about women and that, once it was over, they drank a big glass of milk together while reading the newspaper. The couple begin a discussion, and we are regaled with a string of unrelated anecdotes. We are treated to stories about the English meal, which was really rather good; the death of a certain Parker after an operation; the first anniversary of Bobby Watson's death; the fact that Bobby had married a woman with the same name and had a son who is also called Bobby Watson; and many more.

The Martins are late for dinner. When they finally arrive, they are greeted by the housekeeper, who berates them for being late. Mr. and Mrs. Smith say hello to them and also lecture them for being late, because they have had to postpone dinner. The Martins sit down at the table, facing each other. They have the feeling that they have met before. After a lot of thinking, they realise that they live in the same house and therefore must be married. Happy with this conclusion, they embrace. However, even though everything seems to point to them being married, Mary maintains that this is not the case.

Mrs. Smith tries to start up a conversation by asking her guests if they have any interesting stories from their holidays. It turns out that nothing noteworthy happened, and so Mrs. Martin simply explains the extraordinary event that she saw earlier in the day – she witnessed a man retie his laces. They are all astounded by this story. Each of them then begins to share the strange things, similar to the man retying his laces, which happened to them during the day. Suddenly, the doorbell rings. When Mrs. Smith goes to open the door, there is no one there. She therefore comes back to the table, a little put out. A debate then begins about whether or not there is always someone at the door if the doorbell rings or, on the contrary, if there is never anyone.

The doorbell rings again. This time, the Fire Chief, an old family friend, is there and asks to come in. He greets the Martins and moves to take off his helmet, but refuses to sit down because he is on official business. Finally, he leaves his helmet on and takes a seat. He then begins to complain that there have not been very many fires recently and he does not have very much to do. This is hardly surprising, in his opinion, because the people who are most likely to burn their house down, like match dealers, are insured against fires and therefore never have fires which need putting out. Recognising the chief's voice, Mary suddenly comes into the room and throws her arms around his neck. She is happy to see him because she used to be in love with him. The two lovers' embrace irritates the Martins and the Smiths. The servant is then dismissed to the kitchen and the Fire Chief leaves the guests. Once again finding themselves in a smaller group, the two couples exchange proverbs, ideas and observations, such as: "An Englishman's home is truly his castle", "My uncle lives in the country, but that's none of the midwife's business", "To hell with polishing!" (pp. 38-39).

After this last reply, there is a certain feeling of tension and irritation between the characters. Other absurd phrases in the same style as the previous ones continue to pour out until the end of the play.

When the light comes back on in the theatre, we hear the lines from the first scene for a second time. However, they are no longer read by the Smiths, but by the Martins, who have replaced the first couple in their English living room to smoke their English pipe while reading their English paper.

CHARACTER STUDY

MRS. SMITH

Mrs. Smith is a middle-class English woman married to Mr. Smith, who is also a real middle-class English man. She is the mother of two children, as she mentions in the opening lines of the play. However, they never appear in the play. We find out a bit about them through the stories their parents tell about them.

She is quite a chatty woman and seems to enjoy speaking but not really saying much, as is the case of many of Ionesco's characters. She has a rather strong personality, and gets annoyed at various points throughout the play (she gets angry with her husband, she gets annoyed when nobody is at the door, and she is not at all happy to see that her servant is so close with the Fire Chief).

MR. SMITH

We know very little about Mr. Smith other than the fact that he is English and proud of it, smokes a pipe and likes to read the newspaper. He seems to have a bit of a teasing side to him, since he apparently takes great pleasure in riling up his wife. He also likes contradicting her and discussing trivial things with her.

MRS. MARTIN

Mrs. Elizabeth Martin comes from Manchester in England and is married to Mr. Martin, who comes from the same city. She is middle-class and has a daughter called Alice. Although the little girl never appears in the play, her parents mention her. We know that she has one red eye and one white eye. The couple's house is also briefly described.

MR. MARTIN

There is not really anything more to be said about Mr. Martin than what has already been said about his wife.

MARY

Mary is the Smith family's servant. She is young and energetic. She seems to enjoy going out and having fun, but she also appreciates the simple pleasure of sitting down with a glass of milk in a café to read the newspaper. She has the talent of annoying Mrs. Smith with her upbeat nature, and her employer never tires of making snide remarks about her. Like all English people, she is a stickler for punctuality and scolds the Martins for arriving late. She also had a love affair with the Fire Chief, who she was madly in love with.

THE FIRE CHIEF

The Fire Chief is a prankster who likes to ring people's doorbells and then hide to see their reaction. He is unlucky because he does not have much work to do: fires are becoming less and less common in his sector. Nevertheless, he remains as jovial as ever and continues to regale his hosts with absurd, entertaining stories.

ANALYSIS

THE THEATRE OF THE ABSURD

In the years immediately following the Second World War, a new type of theatre, which was completely different from classical genres, appeared. Several names are used to describe this phenomenon, which is neither a literary school nor a literary movement and which attempts to highlight the absurdity of the human condition (the term absurd meaning "at variance with reason; manifestly false", according to the *Collins English Dictionary*). The expression "Theatre of the Absurd" was first used by the author and critic Jacques Lemarchand (1908-1974). He placed several post-war dramatists, notably Eugène Ionesco, Samuel Beckett (Irish writer, 1906-1989) and Arthur Adamov (French dramatist, 1908-1970), in this genre. The name coined by Lemarchand was later formalised in 1961 thanks to Martin Esslin's essay *The Theatre of the Absurd*. Ten years later, Emmanuel Jacquart published a study on what he called "le théâtre de derision" ("The Theatre of Derision"). Although he was inspired by Esslin's work, Jacquart believed that "absurd" is not the appropriate term because it ignores the humour present in these plays. As well as being described as "absurd" or "derisive", these plays are also sometimes classed as "New Theatre", in reference to the *nouveau roman* ("New Novel"). The *nouveau roman* contrasts with the traditional novel and challenges our idea of plot, character psychology and coherence.

Those young, so-called "absurd" writers were a part of the

avant-garde, which is characterised by a rejection of norms, whether they are societal, political or academic. Their writings were influenced by existentialism, the leading figures of which were Jean-Paul Sartre (1905-1980) and Albert Camus (1913-1960) with his *The Myth of Sisyphus* (1942), subtitled "Essay on the Absurd". This philosophical movement argues that human beings are the only masters of their lives, independent of all philosophical, religious and moral doctrine. In "A Talk about the Avant-Garde", published in *Notes and Counter Notes*, Ionesco explains the particularities of 1950s avant-garde and how he himself found a place in the movement.

> "Indeed, this abandoned avant-garde movement has not been outstripped, but buried by the reactionary return of old dramatic formulas that sometimes dare to pretend they are new ones. The theatre is not of our age. It manifests a dated psychology, the right comedy style, bourgeois prudence and a realism which refuses to be called conventional but which really is, a submission to dogmatism which is a menace to the artist" (pp. 50-51).

Questioning conventions is one of the legacies not only of the Dada and Surrealist movements, but also of the theatre of Alfred Jarry (French writer, 1873-1907) and his famous *Ubu Roi* ("King Ubu", 1896). The denunciation of the absurdity of man's existence and the banality of daily life was already present in this play: "The curtain rises to reveal a scene which is supposed to represent Nowhere [...], just like the action [which] takes place in Poland, a country which is legendary and divided enough to be this Nowhere..."[1] ("Autre presentation d'Ubu roi", *Ubu roi*).

In keeping with this rejction of the established rules and dogmas, Ionesco subtitles *The Bald Soprano* "anti-theatre", even though the text conforms to the codes of theatre: there is a character list, the text is broken up into scenes, the stage directions explain what is happening on stage, dialogues are meant for specific characters, and so on. Paradoxically, he continued to refuse the term of the "absurd", finding it inappropriate to describe the world around him.

> "I prefer the word "unusual" to "absurd". Sometimes the world seems to be empty of all expression, of all content. [...] But what is absurd, or rather what is unusual, is reality more than anything else. I realise that I use the word absurd to express very different notions [...] sometimes I call what I do not understand absurd [...] I also call the man who wanders aimlessly, the man cut off from his essential roots absurd [...] All that is the experience of metaphysical absurdity, of the absolute mystery; then there is the absurd in the form of madness, contradiction, the expression of my discord with the world, with my profound discord with myself, with the discord between the world and itself"[2] (Entre la vie et le rêve. Entretien avec Claude Bonnefoy, "Between life and dreams. Interview with Claude Bonnefoy").

The term of the absurd is supposed to describe the absurdity of the world and, therefore, how it is represented on the stage. However, Ionesco believes that the world is not

---

1. This quotation has been translated by BrightSummaries.com.
2. This quotation has been translated by BrightSummaries.com.

absurd. As a result, his plays, which are supposed to say something about the world, are also not absurd. It is not a question of equivalence (the theatre is the world), but of consequence.

However, the Theatre of the Absurd is not an academic movement with well-defined rules which must be followed. There are instead several common points shared by certain dramatists in the 1950s. We can see some of these in Ionesco's *The Bald Soprano*, which is considered to be the first "absurd" play:

- **The rejection of realism, whether this is in the characters or in the plot**. The characters are archetypes with neither psychology nor depth, to such an extent that they are interchangeable and are even reversed at the end of the play. There is no longer any kind of plot, at least not in the Aristotelian sense of the term, which is to say a series of events, because nothing changes throughout the play. The play simply restarts in an endless cycle. Ionesco notes in his *Journal* that "all intrigue, all particular action is pointless"[3].
- **The denunciation of the absurdity (or the absence of logic) of existence**. In this regard, Ionesco takes a rather existentialist view of the matter. Man is nothing more than nothingness, with no meaning. The author is very familiar with the works of the two main representatives of existentialism, as *Antidotes* and *Notes and Counter Notes* prove. Ionesco had an ambivalent relationship with

---

3. This quotation has been translated by BrightSummaries.com.

Sartre, both admiring his novel *Nausea* and criticising his uncompromising dogmatism, while he had nothing but praise for Camus, and was deeply saddened by his death.

- **The denunciation of the petit bourgeois mentality**. The author sees this mentality as being made up of clichés and conformism, and of being incapable of expressing a distinctive personality.
- **The absence of the meaning of time**. Time has no more meaning, almost as if it is broken, which means the audience is not really sure what time it is in the play. In *The Bald Soprano*, the opening stage directions specify that the clock strikes "17 English strokes" after "a long moment of English silence". Mrs. Smith then comments "There, it's nine o'clock" (pp. 8-9).
- **The absence of the meaning of place**. Just like in Jarry's *Ubu roi*, the action could take place "Nowhere". For postwar dramatists, this is a "refusal to reproduce reality as it is usually perceived, [which] does not cause them to turn their back on it, but allows them to take hold of the material that it offers them to undermine it or illuminate it from within"[4] (Abirached, 1994). For example, in the description of the scenery, the repetition of the word "English" strips it of all meaning. It no longer means anything and becomes, just like the characters, interchangeable. The room could just as easily be Turkish or Italian; the fact that it is English brings nothing to the play.
- **The absence of the meaning of language**. It no longer means anything and only serves to exchange words,

---

4. This quotation has been translated by BrightSummaries.com.

which are themselves meaningless.

THE JEOPARDISING OF LANGUAGE

Because of his experiences, Ionesco was always very passionate when it came to the question of language. Born to a French mother and a Romanian father, he arrived in France when he was only a few years old, but was forced to go back to Romania against his will by his father when he was a teenager. He then had to "relearn" his mother tongue.

The jeopardising of language, considered to be the main characteristic of the Theatre of the Absurd, allows the author to denounce the illusion of interpersonal exchange. Ionesco believes that this impossibility of communication is the very definition of the absurd: "what is sometimes labelled the absurd is only the denunciation of the ridiculous nature of a language empty of substance, sterile, made up of clichés and slogans: of theatre-that-is-known-in-advance" (*Notes and Counter Notes*, p. 46). For Professor Jean-Pierre Ryngaert, Ionesco's language is in fact a dispossession of language. The simple fact of speaking has become a source of anguish.

Consequently, in his *Fragments of a Journal*, Ionesco presents us with his perception of language, the anguish a being feels when he is not in agreement with "his language", and his impression that it has been replaced with a worrying proliferation of clichés. The more humans use clichés, the more they suffocate under their terrifying banality and the more they lose sight of their being. This metaphysical point of view on language (who are we if we are not our language, or if a dead language is imposed on us every time we open our mouths?) is expressed obsessively in all of Ionesco's plays.

As for the dialogues, they are made up of niceties, platitudes and clichéd expressions. At the end of the play, the illusion of the conversation between the characters is replaced with a completely meaningless argument, which has absolutely no logic at all. To create this exchange, Ionesco uses several techniques to deconstruct language:

- **False arguments like sophisms and false analogies**, as in this exchange between the Smiths which comes to an uncertain conclusion:

  > "Mr Smith: A conscientious doctor must die with his patient if they can't get well together. The captain of a ship goes down with his ship into the briny deep, he does not survive alone.
  > Mrs. Smith: One cannot compare a patient with a ship.
  > Mr. Smith: Why not? A ship has its diseases too; moreover, your doctor is as hale as a ship, that's why he should have perished at the same time as his patient, like the captain and his ship.
  > Mrs. Smith: Ah! I hadn't thought of that... Perhaps it is true... And then, what conclusion do you draw from this?
  > Mr. Smith: All doctors are quacks. And all patients too. Only the Royal Navy is honest in England" (p. 11).

- **Tautologies** are used to strip language of its meaning. The characters repeat information which the audience already knows. When Mrs. Smith announces that "Mary did the potatoes very well, this evening. The last time she did not do them so well" (p. 9), the second sentence adds no new information, given that it was already implied with the words "this evening".

- **The falseness of causal links**, in spite of the use of linking words. When Mrs. Smith announces "We've eaten well this evening. That's because we live in the suburbs of London and because our name is Smith" (p. 9), the conjunction "because" implies that the fact of eating well is linked with geographical location. However, it is clear that the two have absolutely no relation to each other.
- **Wordplay**. Take for example this line: "take a circle, caress it, and it will turn vicious" (p. 38); it introduces a pun with the expression "vicious circle".
- **Playing with sounds**. Ionesco makes use of homophony, for example in the following list, which sounds correct but is actually not in the least bit logical: "Yoghurt is excellent for the stomach, the kidneys, the appendicitis and apotheosis" (p. 10) and alliteration (in other words, the repetition of consonants): "the cook beats batter better" (p. 39).
- **The large amount of onomatopoeia,** which replaces language at the end of the play. The characters no longer use phrases following the model "subject, verb, object", but just make isolated sounds.
- **Neologisms** (words invented by the author), like the "cacas" (p. 40) or the "gobblegobblers" (p. 41).
- **The repetition of fixed expressions.** The Martins constantly repeat the words "how curious [...] is" (pp. 15-18).
- **The sudden appearance of French** (or English in the

original French version): "Go take a douche" (p. 40).

- **Contradictions** which sabotage any attempt at reasoning. At the start of the play, the Smiths mention the death of someone they knew, a man called Bobby Watson. They went to his funeral three or four years ago, where they met his wife, who also goes by the name of Bobby Watson. Mr. Smith tries to describe her:

> "Mr. Smith: She has regular features and yet one cannot say that she is pretty. She is too big and stout. Her features are not regular but still one can say that she is very pretty. She is a little too small and too thin. She's a voice teacher.
> [*The clock strikes five times. A long silence.*]
> Mrs. Smith: And when do they plan to be married, those two?
> Mr. Smith: Next spring, at the latest (p. 12).

- **Anecdotes,** which the characters seem to love. However, they are either completely mundane (Mrs. Martin saw a man retie his shoelaces, pp. 21-22) or incomprehensible, like the Fire Chief's "experimental fable" (p. 30).

The title of the text also involves playing with language. It has no relation to the text because the bald soprano is brought up only once and has absolutely no role in the play. The characters mention it quickly, in passing, when the Fire Chief is about to leave:

> Fire Chief [*moving towards the door, then stopping*]: Speaking of that – the bald soprano? [*General silence, embarrassment*]
> Mrs. Smith: She always wears her hair in the same style (p. 37).

Ionesco chose the title precisely because there is no so-prano, bald or otherwise, in the play. He explains in "The Bald Soprano: The Tragedy of Language" that "this detail should suffice" (*Notes and Counter Notes*, p. 177). Ionesco was torn between several possibilities, like *English Without Toil* or *The English Hour*, for a long time. However, it was an actor who accidently gave Ionesco the idea for the title, as Ionesco explains in *Notes and Counter Notes*:

> "There was some passing reference to an 'institutrice blonde,' [and] Henri-Jacques made a mistake and said 'cantatrice chauve.' 'There's the title of the play!' I cried. So that is how *La Cantatrice chauve – The Bald Soprano* – got its name" (p. 183).

A CRITICISM OF THE BOURGEOISIE

The idea to criticise the bourgeois family and values came to Ionesco at the same time as his desire to speak the language of Shakespeare. Feeling that he was a bit limited writing in only French and Romanian, he decided to begin learning a new language and, in order to do so, used the *Assimil* me-thod. This method allows you to gradually learn a language with small grammar and vocabulary lessons in order to better assimilate new knowledge. It also has a conversation guide which is useful for tourists abroad.

It was this manual in particular which interested Ionesco. However, he very quickly lost interest, because it was full of clichés and prejudices on what foreigners look for when they visit England, as well as on what English people say to each other. It served as the basis for the writing of *The Bald*

Soprano, although the play's social critique was levelled at more than just the English middle class.

The beginning of the play is a good example of what Ionesco thinks of the bourgeoisie: people completely indifferent to one another who live parallel lives even when they are in the same room (Mr. Smith ignores Mrs. Smith even though she is talking directly to him), symbolising the superficiality of bourgeois relationships. The characters are proud that they are bourgeois because they enjoy the good things in life that this status gives them. They even begin to think that they deserve these advantages: "There, it's nine o'clock. We've drunk the soup, and eaten the fish and chips, and the English salad. The children have drunk English water. We've eaten well this evening. That's because we live in the suburbs of London and because our name is Smith" (p. 9).

These characters are difficult to pin down, and make absurd conversation, contradict themselves, get angry, insult each other, and so on, which makes real communication difficult. This type of closed discussion is doomed to failure, and is exactly the impression Ionesco has of the bourgeoisie. Indeed, the bourgeoisie forget essential things (who they are married to, for example) and only remember what is relatively unimportant (like the minor details of what they have done or what they have eaten). The author also highlights their stupidity through their appalled reactions when they see 'normal' people doing simple things (for example, a man in the street bending over to tie his shoelaces).

The bourgeoisie are seen as all being cast in the same mould, with each of them having the same appearance and characteristics. This can be seen particularly in the passage about Bobby Watson: his aunt and uncle are both called Bobby Watson, as are his wife and two children. The fact that they have all been given the same name highlights that they are similar to such an extent that it is difficult to differentiate them. As for the Martins and the Smiths, they have no other identity than "Mr./Mrs., husband/wife of". This is why they do not have their own personality.

THE RECEPTION OF THE PLAY

The public did not know how to take the play when it was first staged in 1950. With its non-communication, absence of plot and characters as well as the unflattering representation of the bourgeoisie, they wondered if they were being made fun of. A lot of people who saw the play were convinced that it would quickly be forgotten, and theatregoers were torn between laughing at this "anti-play" and walking out. Ionesco was very troubled to hear laughter, because he thought he had written a "tragedy about language".

In his article "My Critics and I", published in 1956 and included in *Notes and Counter Notes*, Ionesco exposed the paradoxes of his critics who found him talented (or not), funny (or not), both realistic and metaphysical, and so on. The author did not really know what to think:

> "Choosing [a critic] at random, I read each of his reviews as they appeared: he blamed my drama for being too facile, for having no secrets; two months later, the same critic objected to an overloading of heavy and obscure symbols" (*Notes and*

Counter Notes, p. 85).

The difficulty in describing his play led critics to write contradictory things about it, which, at the end of the day, made them into absurd writers. The irony of the situation became more and more evident as time passed. In spite of the numerous criticisms of the play when it was first staged, *The Bald Soprano* returned in 1957 and finally became a runaway success. It has played in the Théâtre de la Huchette ever since and holds the world record for the play that has been staged continuously in the same theatre for the longest time, which makes the play the theatre's speciality.

Ionesco's work has achieved worldwide success. The most prestigious reward the dramatist received was no doubt his election to the Académie française in 1970 to the position previously held by Jean Paulhan, who was a great admirer of his work.

FURTHER REFLECTION

SOME QUESTIONS TO THINK ABOUT...

- How can the title of the play be explained? In your opinion, does it sum up the play well?
- Do the characters each have their own distinct personality? Explain your answer.
- In what way is the play a satire of the bourgeoisie and its values?
- Do you think that the play is more like a comedy or a tragedy? Similarly, is it optimistic or pessimistic, in your opinion?
- What is the difference between the Theatre of the Absurd and more conventional theatre such as, for example, the plays of Corneille (1606-1684), Molière (1622-1673), or Racine (1639-1699)? Conversely, do they have any similarities? Explain your answer.
- Do you think that the Theatre of the Absurd could have existed in the 17th century? Why?
- Do you think that the absurd could be present in a form of art other than theatre? Justify your answer.
- Do you think that the Theatre of the Absurd can say anything about modern times? If so, explain what and how.
- The Theatre of the Absurd developed after the Second World War. Place it within the historical context of the time.
- Compare *The Bald Soprano* to other absurd plays such as *The Lesson* by Ionesco or *Waiting for Godot* by Samuel Beckett (1906-1989). Highlight the similarities and the differences between these works.

We want to hear from you!
Leave a comment on your online library
and share your favourite books on social media!

FURTHER READING

REFERENCE EDITION

- Ionesco, E. (1982) *The Bald Soprano & Other Plays*. Trans. Allen, D. New York: Grove Press.

REFERENCE STUDIES

- Abirached, R. (1994) *La crise du personnage dans le théâtre moderne*. Paris: Gallimard.
- Cash, J. (2015) Theatre of the Absurd Conventions. *The Drama Teacher*. [Accessed 7 April 2017]. Available from: <http://www.thedramateacher.com/theatre-of-the-absurd-conventions/>
- Ionesco, E. (1996) *Entre la vie et le rêve. Entretien avec Claude Bonnefoy*. Paris: Gallimard.
- Ionesco, E. (1964) *Notes and Counter Notes*. Trans. Allen, D. New York: Grove Press.
- Jarry, A. (1972) *Œuvres completes*. Paris: Gallimard.

ADAPTATION

The Bald Soprano was staged for the first time in le théâtre des Noctambules in Paris on 11 May 1950. The play was directed by Nicolas Bataille, who made only very minor changes in order to keep the essence of Ionesco's work. Nevertheless, in spite of this precaution, the performances were not met with a great deal of enthusiasm, and the press tore Ionesco to shreds, seeing him as nothing more than a mocking, bourgeoisie-hating writer.

The play was only fully appreciated many years later. It is still staged regularly in theatres worldwide to this day.

MORE FROM BRIGHTSUMMARIES.COM

- Reading guide – *Exit the King* by Eugène Ionesco.
- Reading guide – *Rhinoceros* by Eugène Ionesco.

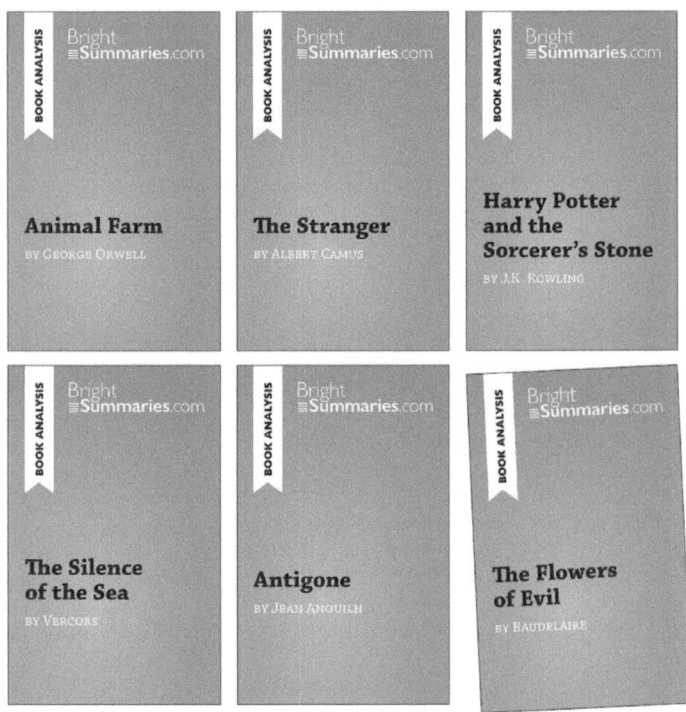

www.brightsummaries.com

Ebook EAN: 9782806296641

Paperback EAN: 9782806296658

Legal Deposit: D/2017/12603/224

This guide was written with the collaboration of Johanna Biehler for the chapters 'The Theatre of the Absurd', 'The jeopardising of language' and 'The reception of the play'.

Cover: © Primento

Digital conception by Primento, the digital partner of publishers.

This guide was produced with the support of the *Service Général des Lettres et du Livre of the* Wallonia-Brussels Federation.